THE STONE SHIP

Other poetry by Danielle Hope

Fairground of Madness
– with Shirley Barker
(Rockingham, 1992)

City Fox
(Rockingham, 1997)

Danielle Hope

The Stone Ship

Rockingham Press

Published in 2003 by
The Rockingham Press
11 Musley Lane,
Ware, Herts SG12 7EN
www.rockinghampress.com

British Library Cataloguing-in-Publication Data

A catalogue record for this book
is available from the British Library

ISBN 1 873468 91 1

Printed in Great Britain
by Biddles Limited
Guildford & King's Lynn

The royalties of this book are being donated to
Survivors Poetry
"promoting poetry by survivors of mental distress"
Diorama Arts Centre,
34 Osnaburgh Street,
London NW1 3ND

Acknowledgments

Acknowledgements are due to the editors of: *Acumen, Fire, The Interpreter's House* and *The Poet's Voice*; and of the anthologies, *Home* (Katabasis Press, London, 1999), *Selected Poets of the United Kingdom* (Spiny Babbler, Nepal, 2000), *Caliban in Prague* (Tempest Poets, 2001), *The Kent and Sussex Poetry Competition Anthology* (2001), *Torriano Poets* (Hearing Eye 2003), and *Work* (Katabasis Press, London, 2000) in whose pages some of these poems first appeared.

'Application' was a prizewinner in The Housman Society Poetry Competition (2000), judged by U.A. Fanthorpe and Anthony Thwaite.

'Tomorrow it will be Management Consultants' won second prize in the Pitshanger Poets National competition (2001) judged by Alan Brownjohn.

Thanks are also due to Douglas Clark for hosting some on my poems on his web pages, at: *www.bath.ac.uk/~exxdgdc*.

I thank my fellow members of the Tempest Poets for the critique of individual poems, and Jane Kirwan, Patricia Oxley and William Oxley for helpful comments on the whole manuscript.

Contents

Postcard from Van Gogh
to John Russell

Some would consider this a lazy
way to paint. No need to offer wine,
coffee, even water. No cost of a model.
No rearrangements. No unexpected
complaints. And I am not tired.

A face, left and right swapped.
Scars newly seen.
Self-portrait. Or mask.
Not like Gauguin, he drew me
'dead tired and emotionally terrible'

taking so long in painting
that the sunflowers died.
Or you Russell, making me out
the grand master, in a brown suit
holding a pencil. The serious artist

scrutinising his work. No, I am
a clutch of greedy brushes
a wild pallet of colour
sculpting my hungry ghost.

Learning a Language

I walk to the woodland
to seek shapes
in moss stained on trees.
But there is no tapestry.
Only bark that is hard
a trail of straw footsteps
in the weave of dead leaves
and sunlight
a path that disappears.

I walk to the canal
to catch words in water
before they splash over lock
and drill stone.
But even if I take a stick
and trouble the glaze with my name
ripples remain unintelligible.
A coot swims crooked circles
under a pulsing bridge.

Is it that this language is indistinct?
Or am I blind
unable to tell line
from shadow, green from grey?
Or both?
Uneasy travellers
destined to read different alphabets
draw arrow as sail-boat
twenty types of twilight
discerned as one.

And I walk to the sea
to look for messages in dunes
and sea-grass
but find a tangle of red flowers I cannot identify.
The sea shuffles
illegible scatters of sand.

Visitor

When the clock grows quiet
and I have changed into evening
you come into the room soft
as moonrays that light
the back of my arms.

'How have you been?'
you ask, as the cat springs
from your favourite chair
so we can break bread over
midnight conversation.

Building a Snowman

First time south of the border, I write to you.
The pencil point scratches my tongue-tip.
Words are elusive and rickety
as the snowman we built last thaw.
On television a man gently explains
the need to reward risk. With money.
Properly. He wears a charcoal suit,
a blue tie, a smile, perfect teeth.
I wonder if he had plastic surgery.

Then there are the advertisements –
charities with life-saving treatments,
the cleanest washing soap,
a rescue operation in Africa, the ring
of your mobile phone, how to get rich.
Our hands froze building the snowman –
yet his hat flattened his coal eye,
his arms never emerged, legs collapsed.
How do I tell you that here car emissions
and beggars fill the streets.
Last year we never believed
that the snowman could be built.

A Trail of Stones

The first time she did not realise.
No guards. No check point.
No snipers posted in blank flats.
No queue shuffling forward.
No body search or sniffer dogs.
No passport required.

Later – like the leak suddenly spotted
by its stain in the ceiling, or the death
of a friend by a letter coming back –
she recognised she had crossed
to another country in the time taken
to push open a door.

So much the same, so much different.
Her tongue coiling in a strange
language, eyes misreading Made
for Mad. Always late, lost, the clasp
of her bag fallen open, her hair unravelled.
A genial people, giving generous food and wine
but also judging speech and silence
in prisons the tourists do not visit.

I do not belong. But three weeks later
she returns clutching fake papers.
East winds howl on the back of her neck.
Winter falls as she lays a trail of stones to find home.
And over months, like a llama crossing
mountains, time and again she picks a path
from one country to the other, grown sure-footed.
Now she says: *it is like changing clothes
only what you shed is skin, a swift re-arrangement
of hair, the turn of your face.*

Double agent, fighter for the resistance
she knows routes across the border
and the way from one self to the next.
But in her nightmares she wakes
and calls out in the wrong language
or loses the path of stones back
or fails to find the woman she left behind.

Providing

Life assurance
payable on death
providing it is swift and from
a new unexpected illness.

Mortgage protection plan
payable for one of twenty ailments
providing that it is incurable,
uncomplicated, unrelated to profession,
psychology, diet, drink or lifestyle,
or injury, infection, infarct or inflammation,
is not inherent, dormant, or inborn
being absent in your siblings, parents,
grandparents, aunts, cousins, children,
and is claimed before sixty.

Nursing home protection cover
payable for a place in
one of our deluxe nursing homes –
providing that there are
no relatives to care for you,
no local authority homes,
you are incapacitated and incompetent
(but not incontinent)
your entry is involuntary
and does not occur before eighty-five.

Premium waiver indemnity
payable if your premiums are late
except in cases of insolvency.

A benefit may be deducted
from a previous benefit.
Persons excluded: fire-eaters,
ski-instructors, explorers,
builders, window-cleaners,
divers, astronauts,
publicans, poisoners,
pilots,
painters,
poets.

Today it is Management Consultants

Thursday afternoon. You sit
in a blue anorak among
twenty-five scarecrow allotments
puddled by weeds. Dogs and blackbirds
shower soil on winter paths.
Six mallards string across the sky
the colour of slugs.

Yesterday it was production.
You scrutinised the prospectus
written for weary soil, struggled
to grow tomatoes bigger than raisins
matchstick beans, unripe
raspberries smelling of weak tea.

Today they arrive in shiny wellingtons
tramp the walkways over twine and hedge-rose
ankled in brown generous mud.
Such poor soil, no surprise –
couldn't call these harvests.
Spend an hour tutting to their pens
by the mangy broccoli.

Adventurous to try broccoli here
in a north wind so near Preston.
You imagine their houses.
Habitat sofa, soft-tone lamps
a microwave in every kitchen.
Today it is management consultants.
Yesterday it was production.
Tomorrow it will be downsizing.

Then the hail begins.
Magpies get the best of it.
On the stream bank, at the edge
of the allotments, they hop
and peck at tuna paste sandwiches.
In the North wind
a white tablecloth flaps.

On Course

Two professors and their students
sit drinking on the terrace.
Their vodka blood is a delicacy
for mosquitoes and night flies.
The moon is almost full. Laughter
is wood smoke rising.

Across weather fronts I imagine you now,
broad fingers turning the pages
of Camus. Then rising, creak
of floorboard, click into darkness.
Through the window, in the cobalt
bath of sky, the moon rolls
above town lights. Your scent
lingers in the silent room.

The White Duck that Thinks it's a Heron

is poised in the shallow water watching
for fish. *Duck you are no heron*
you should eat algae and weed, not fish.

But each morning, after the great heron
has robbed the river's flood then
spiralled away over wrath-faced fishermen,
the white duck waddles forward.

It catches nothing. Except the scorn
of walkers and three bold women
from the canoeing club who test currents
where stream permeates sea, navigate

a family of mallards. Unbroken
through the burn of sun, the white
duck haunts shallow water, watching.
Its own shadow shining and still.

Application

Sirs

Please find enclosed one computer generated
application
for a knighthood. I have carefully observed

your deadline, included as requested a coupon
from the Sunday Times
plus supporting statements from six close chums.

Encourage the panel to forgive
my signature.
Not yet sufficiently distinguished.

But in time I promise to make
my sur-name
seem double-barrelled.

I practise hinting that daddy walked
grouse moors
rather than an allotment.

The idea of window tables in restaurants
is attractive
or the inspector on the train *agreeing*

the queue was too tedious for me to buy
a ticket –
Fat credit at the bank

no waiting at the doctors' surgery.
A smart seat
at the opera, hot American enthusiasm.

But it's not only for these. Honest. It would boost
your political quota.
And if your worst objection is tokenism

I'll accept being a token. And at least
no one will ever
again ask, is it Mrs, Miss or Ms?

The Art of Lending Umbrellas

In mid June on the hottest day
of the year Joan rushes out
to lend me her umbrella.
She has been doing this since May
but today is special – the loan is free.
Inspect this new shiny black
automatic, caress
the lion head handle.
I glance down at my grubby toes
in open sandals, newly
shaved legs, white shorts
green shirt. *See these*
special rates, remember
the risk of summer shower.

Come October, the first cloudburst
and I won't be able to find her.
Ringing her bell for hours
a cold burn of water on my neck
to be told by her ugly brother
that all umbrellas are out.
Rates are double. Hair sodden
damp oozing onto my feet.
At the back door a river of people
returning reluctant umbrellas.
The rate has risen. Joan
lending umbrellas in Java.

Joan in Pormoskki Forest

At the concert, Joan can tell cello
from double base, cornet, tuba,
trombone, viola, violin, piccolo,
flute, baritone, alto, tenor.

In the forest, Joan can tell chaffinch
from thrush, bee, blackbird, tree sparrow
robin, wren, woodpecker, cuckoo,
blue tit, rook, partridge.

Where are the ushers, seat rows,
ice-creams, programmes?
Have they finished tuning up yet?
Where is the conductor?

Certainty

Let us begin with a death.
Perhaps it is murder.
A bloody knife on a table
A body lying in the middle
of the room, vigorous
photographers and policemen,
one fingerprint in the dust
evidence that hardens piece by piece
until 'Where were you between
ten and midnight?

Step closer. A Victorian-long winter
a one bar fire, frost imitating
stained glass, snow blaze
on pavements, local shops shuttered
cheese patterned with mice.
Prices rise, savings fall,
shares disappear.
A credit bureau refuses.
The bank manager's regretful smile.

Any Questions

What did you do, brave or otherwise
to deserve this veneer and walnut?
Your room stretches like an opulent continent.
      But it's only a rooftop Portacabin
      built to last five years. Already it creaks
      in a high wind and mould spoils the leather.

Oh it's a pleasant sail to the private wing
past Monet prints provided by Heritage Lottery.
They enhance the hospital environment.
      And through wide windows the Thames
      is romantic in rain, grey sand shifts
      against banks as the muddy barges pass.

The arches of Westminster hide
cardboard men on Hungerford Bridge.

The Thunderbolt's Training Manual

Choose a soporific afternoon. As sunbathers
doze, saturday papers abandoned.
Smell suntan oil among rhododendrons.
Drone of bee and walkman.

Circle a breeze about marshy thighs.
Cloud the sky. Start far off. Slowly.
Observe how sheep know better
set their rumps to the wind.

Enjoy sound. A long peal
a blast of cathedral bells. Crash.
Enjoy light flashed on dark.
Newspapers speared on the rose bush.

Relish the sunbathers' scatter.
Listen to dogs bark and bark and bark.
Send a drop of rain.
Send a canyon of rain.

How to Swim with Sharks

After Voltaire Cousteau

Rule 1. Assume all fish are sharks until proven otherwise

Do you imagine a shark
will sail towards you wearing
a gaudy neon sign

'I AM A SHARK'?
Masters of disguise
they simulate playful dolphins

even fur seals, tucking
their fins down
hiding their wolf teeth.

Innocent tiny fish
may become sharks
as they grow.

Rule 2. Do not bleed

Apparently imperative.
Difficult.

Wounds have a nasty habit of bleeding
and non-bleeding wounds are unhealthy
being breeding grounds
for festering sores, septicaemia, decay.

But blood brings more sharks –
is to be discouraged
if possible prevented
at least delayed.

**Rule 3. Counter aggression
with a sharp bop on the nose**

Noses are sensitive objects
and Mr Cousteau asserts
that a sharp blow to the nose
counters the exploratory
action which precedes an attack.

Never having courage
enough to bop a real shark
on the nose – I worry that
the nose is uncannily close
to the mouth.

Rule 4. Disorganise an organised attack

This is my favoured option.
Distraction or internal dissension
leads sharks to forget why
they approached.

At best it could cause
random lashing of tails
an exhausting activity
or attack of each other.

Rule 5. Build a bridge or hire a boat

Not being so charmed by water
as Mr Cousteau, I added this.
Providing that sharks cannot
climb the bridge or sink the boat

we could cross without getting wet.
The only problem is to divert
the sharks and to ensure there
are no python or pterodactyls.

Rhino on the 9.15 to Watford

I am a poem and I dislike Actors
lurching towards me with their sonorous

vowels and articulated consonants –
a late train jerking into a siding

wheels squeal, shriek tut
as it stops, with hoot, shunt, halt.

The rhythm of carriages
bounce over connections

thunderous thuds on the points.
And all that projection. A rhino

on board, paces its cage, hoofs
clump on wooden floors, one horn

rattles iron bars, waving
a tormented gesture from Henry V.

A carefully guided missile
missing its target.

Form versus Poetry

Constructing perfect rhymes
Joan abolishes all meaning

the verse pedestal worshipped.
After death she will be recalled

as an ugly old woman walking
backwards on an ugly concrete road.

Her instructions: ashes to be scattered
in perfect pentameters.

Reasons

It was the train
the wrong sort of rain
the bus was late
it wouldn't wait
never came.

It was the door
so insecure
the lack
of window locks
they had more.

It was his walk
that lilting talk
his stare
the colour of his hair
he'd got work.

It was the dress
pulled tight across
her hips
those strawberry lips
her giddiness.

It was the flesh
moaning on the Net
no risk
to download onto disk
my palms sweat.

It was the snake.

Mountains

My neighbour Joan, came
over yesterday, to discuss anything
except the mountain
that has grown
at the bottom of her garden.

First, there were two clods of earth.
Joan trod them flat
with her second-best winter boots.
But a week later
a small column sprouted –

has been swelling since.
But she is not worried
doesn't believe the chatter –
those who maintain
it's a spacecraft, from galaxy

QR-578, light centuries beyond
our most sensitive radar.
Joan dreads journalists' questions:
What are its plans? Will it poison
the neighbourhood?

Is it the barbarians again –
those always just over the wall?
Responsible for the failure of crops
the sullying of sons and shops –
plotting our downfall

to whom governments deposit
and withdraw ambassadors.
Of course, there won't be a siege
although Joan hoards canned fruit
and canapes, in case.

The Warrior King

after Miro

Three women are interlocked plates
one clutches a spoon
one a hook

one clangs a vacant bowl
her right arm
a broom.

Next a crowned head.
Four stakes slot into steel handcuffs
a comb instead of a brain

a pump-handle nose
one eye protrudes, the other
is a copper saucer.

Then aliens arrive at the exhibition
hurrying as shadows lengthen
across their pale biscuit scented skin.
Last admission is squeaked on the board.
They pay their dues, allocate the figures,
copy fronts, peer behind
trace Miros' star scratched in bronze.

Taking their notes home
this they explain
is how humans see.
Often birds land on their heads.

A man is two right footprints
fixed to an empty cardboard box.
An oily feather ticks.

A warrior is a concrete mixer
spitting spikes, pegs and nails.

The warrior king
is the front door of a house.

Poker Player

Helen's not much good
at this game.
Cards to her chest

she longs to declare
all, compare aces
before she begins.

From her baggy sleeve
cards have a habit
of falling out.

She'd prefer chess.
All those moves
in black or white

the advantage only
for the one
who moves first

the wit on the board
noonday
cunning of the horse.

All pieces exposed
playing a game
of their own making.

Psyche

I'm not a bit like Eve.
No matter what
they say down the market
catch me listening to a snake.
This was different.

It's natural to want
to glimpse the chap
I'm in bed with.
Avid candle wax
sprayed his shoulder.
He woke, was off.
Just like the rest.

Easier to seem helpless –
grin at his mother,
accept tasks, struggle
at sorting seedlings
drown rows of plants
carry her wool cardigan
wash, dust, iron.

Then, Eros came back
to fight grand goats and such.
His dad took my side.
Wish now I'd stood
out for a better house
a bit further away.

But it's that coat hanger Jung
I can't stand. All that
about feminine natures.
Today, with an assertiveness course,
a mobile and a bit of self-defence
I'd be alright. Maybe.

I Knew Her

She made
the newspaper headline
'Sensational Suicide'.

One blizzard night
my greedy troubles hustled
me to her door. There
in the lavender room
lined with lace, it was warm.
'Tell me' said her mauve eyes
'Go on' hummed her ears

among crowded prints
walls buckled by apricot cupboards
her cherry nails ablaze
against a new vase
from Chapel market.
Each hour an avalanche –
trouble, pain, despair.
Each second, each nod, each smile,
she grew smaller
and smaller.

Your Desk

for William Oxley

I had not expected the view.
First, a privet hedge leads
to earthy allotments; string marks
columns of cabbages, a wheelbarrow
upturned, corrugated fencing
a greenhouse, one pane gone.
Behind the hedge, rhubarb mixes
with hawthorn. Then water.
I cannot see the cliff – it falls
faster than the seagull dives.
Instead, the sun of forsythia
twists up to the grey of sea
windless, barely shimmering,
a whole bay of it, and beyond
the arc of Broadsands, Goodrington
Paignton, Torquay. Then a red sea-wall,
white houses and along the ridge
trees spaced like soldiers
against the first rim of clouds.

Your chair has a strong back.
I press my shoulders into it
swivel left and right, move
forward the date on your calendar
discover the cassette tapes
I did not expect you to have.
How slowly the clouds revolve
white, ivory, grey, shadowing
patches of blue gradually bigger.
White houses on the hill
blossom on the blackthorn
for one moment, sunlight
grips the wheelbarrow.

Steam Journey

My grandmother said
sit with your back to the engine
so smoke won't mark your skin
not knowing trains went electric.

Is that why my mother, brother, I
gazing back at sheep above Galmpton
perfect worrying about what is gone
ferries crossed and not crossed

yearn to erase words, payments
cowslip extinction, all embarrassments –
fail to spot hemlock and orchid
flood the track ahead?

Crossings

for PJ

I crossed the sea in a stone ship
a wasteland was the foremast
with girders and bolts below.
When the skies grew choppy
and the sea swelled
our captain braided the wheel tight
roped the breeze in steel
Hail bruised on the catwalk. No stars in sight.
Cromarty gale force ten soon.
A mustard windcheater
scoured my neck.

You crossed the sea in a pleasure boat
Patrick in red on the bow.
Geraniums and violets bobbed in the windows.
Nudging canals or a serene river
pausing at November piers –
ten pins all afternoon
a packet of cigarettes won –
as the shadows grew.
All night guitar chords climbed
to stars and pink lanterns.
Cromarty gale force ten soon.

So how did you die, found fallen alone,
at the base of a stairwell
a discarded maid's entrance
a cheap hotel in the red-light zone?
Discovered frozen, by two morning lovers.
No-one knows how you arrived
fell over the locked gate. Tripped, chased?
A few flowers with messages are already decaying.
A woman leans from the window
What are you here for?

Potato

There are those who find inspiration
in crisp mown hay
or apples sharp and green.

When they speak
words lap along pathways
lined with mint and marigolds

fuchsias nod red diamond heads
and under a silver birch
a mistle thrush calls.

For others the journey
is rock riddled
at the end a towering cliff

a chalk wall.
In poor shade
a potato struggles to bud.

The Move

These rooms are naked except
for the curtains and blinds
I am leaving behind.
Tonight in the dark the walls
will murmur to themselves
while my ghost merges with women
from 1908 who ached in the harness
of rimpled dresses.
A helicopter circles the street.

In the bedroom I stare at the shadow
where the mirror was, search
for champagne times. Car lights
flare across the ceiling.
I touch a last picture, a stone
from the Berlin Wall, the wound
in the door where years ago a stranger
took an axe. There are stains still
from those leaks in the roof. Souvenirs
of bad times are the hardest to leave.
The helicopter circles again.

Through the window
beyond black drizzled pavements
my neighbour's garden is empty
no barbecues, no fireworks.
November leaves blow over the path.
Someone has mended the fence.
I snap out the last light.
Listen at the half-closed door.

Swallow

Black hazard of flight
zigzagging over waterlogged fields
sheep snatching at mud and grass root.
Then a loop over the barn
plunge and skim above tarmac
this arrow pierces the air above the door.
Hidden among dusty beams
last year's nest.

One has returned.
Though dawn drags with cloud
and puddles thicken the yard.
The dry nest viewed from all sides
straw pulled, rearranged.
The cat licks it paws.
It is only a few random
first twigs gathered
not yet a shape.

A Kind of Progress

Nights after school he left
the tea-table early and crept upstairs
to weld a grey box, big as a Wendy house.
Twisted red tubers of wire. Smell of solder.
Snap of a switch and it crackled alive.
Peering over his shoulder I watched him tap
amber words into its flickering screen.
That's BASIC, FORTRAN, C. It added,
subtracted, divided, did algebra, calculus,
we played numbers night after night.

Now fans hum slowly as we hunch beside
smaller grey shells, colour screens,
or press buttons in our palms.
We record, measure, zoom, minimise,
test new ways to count familiar problems,
copy viruses, accidental bugs or programmes
to simulate the building of homes,
reconstruction of bones
total destruction of trees
or explore different routes to Coventry.

The Alternative History
of Jemima Puddle-Duck

So much worse this century than the last
you claim over *canard au gratin* in Camden
Somme, Gallipoli, Blitzkreig, Belsen.
How eagerly we assent you are right –
recall Boers, Jews, Muslims who stormed and died
concentrated in camps. Final primitive
forests are razed, whales fail, ice-caps dissolve,
offices tower, tramps clutter the road.

It's late, my car
weaves home; rain pebbles the windscreen.
Another wrong turn and lost on route.
Last century my same-age ancestor
was already dead, in childbirth or rape
fought forgotten wars, cholera, starvation.
No Beatrix Potter values by the kitchen fire.

The Road Not Seen

after Robert Frost

Is this the road I had hoped to find
    turn left, left, left – seeking a way
out of this dammed yellow wood?
    Lost, looking for any route to squash –
grassed, barely worn, or wildly
    grown. Doomed I take another round.

Or is this the road I never imagined?
    Its existence not even a flash
in a dream, too busy contemplating
    how bees suck at purple buddleia –
and the tragedy, seeing nothing
    but bracken towers above the path.

Advance Directive

Starting late, let mourners gather
on the heath like dandelion down
at noon. Dressed in purple
of thistle, nightshade berry black.
Scarves and gloves red as a poppy.
Let poets organise the funeral today.

Then there will be a reading
moulded for the moment of grief.
Auden's clock materialises soundlessly
steals from room to room, ballads
on the departed, written yesterday
by hands and eyes red as a poppy.

Long poems on loss, short poems,
a deserted desk, epigrams
haiku, words that scatter like ashes
shaken out of the warm urn and blown
across the heath with dandelion down.
Let poets organise the funeral today.

Let them fill the stinging nettle spaces
between conversation, argue theology
plan the wake, drink an estuary of wine
uncover life's kernel, the finished
and unfinished philosophy;
hands and eyes red as a poppy.

But what breathed before
this directive? Too many days
tumbled down, fallen from
dandelion hands, spite
of purple, poison of nightshade
skin red as a poppy.

Eric at the Movies

Eric is telling me about
the latest film at the National –
the Italian resistance. In the end
the priest dies. Painfully.
It is hopeless. Truthful.
And I am angry.
Why are my hands so soft?
Perfume sleeps on my wrist.
Rolls thicken my shoulders
my waist lolls like washing strung
out on a wax dawn.

Outside the taxis are all tangled up
raincoats stand on street corners
or flood from the dimly lit
tube station of Kentish Town.
I imagine walking the streets, watched
and watching, jumping at the tick
of a clock or a certain look.
In torture, it is a luxury to faint.
*'The gentleman has sat so long
on the fence, that the rust
has entered his soul'* mis-quotes Eric.

When even parking-tickets wound, how
could I have stood against the slow
stripping of hunger. Or pain.
Or stared into the eye of a gun.
Offering no more than to run
like the physicists,
who made the bomb
to greet the enemy
that would have killed them.

Amwell Cemetery

Approach behind the church
scale moss stuccoed steps.
Thighs ache. A place for silence.
Earth once disturbed grasses over.
A pot of lemon primula
blooms for this season.
Within the divided yew
a sparrow pipes.

              The dead
lie under their inscriptions.
Last greetings to Arnold
beloved grandfather, father, husband.
Gladys Jane, sister. Some died
but most fell asleep, passed
away, passed on, went home.
Departed this world. The

manner of death unimportant
except for Kate – lost at sea –
Alice run over by a motor vehicle
Frank succumbed to diabetes.
A place for silence.
Steps dull – no steel staircase
or rapid heels. No rattle
of breakfast or cindered

toast, no rank of beds, each
under different instructions –
nil by mouth, awaiting X-ray
coal-tar dressing, light diet only.

Alcohol restricted. Visitors
come and go. And all night Cathy
pipes 'who stole.. who stole..
mother's silver cutlery'.

Headstones huddle like shoppers
under a bus shelter in rain.
Those who never spoke are head
to foot. With inscriptions faded
the old dead make space for the new
dead, stack against a wall.
Among plastic flowers
a stubborn rose trails.

Cockington Boundary

Two ditches   of midge-petalled
water laze   in this dell
islanded between   ancient oaks.

This boundary   marks parish
from parish,   owner
from owner   each side

branded   like numbers
scorched on   the white
rumps   of sheep.

But oaks have crumbled, bridged
the hollows, the partition hidden, as reeds jungle, sycamores
burgeon, new roots tangle through red soil. Badgers slide
between foxgloves, bats swoop,
                    in this unclaimable corridor.

Metier

I recognise the women of King's Cross
by their bare legs and denim skirts –
chalk under sky in alabaster light
outside the seven eleven.
Or crow-black leather, V cut
to the waist, paste face,
blood lips broad as kerbstones.
Uniform of business.

An olive green pendant swings
to the wind above her laced top
as she leans to a steel shutter
speaks to a face I cannot see.
Car lights flash like bleached teeth.
Among leaves under rust-red blankets
two boys and a razer-boned dog beg.
Voices of water.

February squalls newspapers
and cigarette boxes, spears
the slate sky inside my coat
as I thread through beer cans
and look-up at yellow lamps,
pizza shops, smoky office windows,
reflecting traffic all one way.
There are no stars at King's Cross.

Love Song to Coldharbour Lane

Cross wide chestnut water
between Westminster and St Paul's
with business boats tugging
tourists, commuters, wood and steel.

Chug over Blackfriars, gaze at
Tower Bridge, burn breaks downhill.
Low flats gape into carriages
then the Elephant rises, pink and grand.

Houses flatten, runts
of their north Thames sisters;
Edwardian bricks slim and pale
iron boot scrapers for a lean foot.

Between bombed in mousy blocks
backs of warehouses and stacks
of cars awaiting the crush, the roads
maze, potholes deeper than Camden.

Descend at the graffi-green sign
where four railways cross but only
one dare stop, the video shop
shuttered by day, a shooting

or knifing each week. Where north
and east winds battle among fast-stepped
travellers and schoolgirls with battered bags
who gather by Jonnie's for bacon baps.

Outside beer-damp pages of *South London
Shopper* stick to your shoes. *Peg's Furniture*
displays six chairs and a scuffed lime
and cherry chequered sofa, all fourth hand.

In two minutes the train rattles on
towards chestnut trees and the emerald avenues
of Herne Hill and Dulwich. Carries
the paprika air of Coldharbour Lane.

Blackpool Sands

Low winter sun lights sea foam
as it snakes over sand.
Plovers peck in the retreating tide.
At the tram-stop shelter
Time is a limited commodity
in modern life is graffitied in blue
between the Samaritans' notice
and passports for animals.
Old newspapers in the corner breathe.

Shows on the pier are boarded
Frank Dawson's wigwam is closed.
Open-all-year-round shops offer
10 sticks of sugar rock to the pound.
Quidsave sells cheap trays and tin tacks
last year's Christmas candles, cards
tool sets, tinsel, odd socks.
Life is a limited commodity
in modern times the tramlines mutter.
Sixty-six and house shouts the Bingo caller.

As the evening settles into umbrella grey
hotels compete half-broken neon signs
Carlton House, Balmoral View, Cliff,
The Sheraton Rest, Dorchester Sands.
BLA PO   say the summer storm-busted
lights. BLA PO   in red then green
as winter sale shoppers steam
to the top deck of the tram.
Far out to sea a small plane loops.
Plovers peck the retreating tide.
A commodity. Time.

Wind Night

Street lamps tremble.
Clear plastic tangos
across the street
while clouds reel
and the 17 bus
three-quarters empty
rests on Caledonian Road.

In the Texaco station
petrol mists the forecourt.
A lazy customer slouches
from the Ethiopian restaurant.
Outside APKs two Turks
unload water melons
heap them in racks
beside rebuilt fridges
and gas cookers.
A fox barks.

The night sways
in a bad bolero
leaving bruised toes
and torn satin
across the floor –
rattles shuttered shops
padlocks on the canal gates
and the sleepy moorhen's nest –

blows the scent of you
from the open warm window
your silhouette
beside open curtains.

Lungsham Temple

Enter by the waterfall.
The door on the right wakes
your dragons for good luck.
Jostle from Saturday evening
dawning as heat fades, a dustcart
that croons like an ice-cream van
shoppers and drinkers who compete
with scooters pavement-parked
like horses at a race.
The right door.
Inside is as crowded as out.
Men shuffle cards as if painted by Cezanne
a woman clasps an aching foot.
Children run tag, armfuls
of incense glow in orange bowls
smoke circles your throat
singes your eyes.

Hands together, bow.
Whether it is Tao or Buddha
no one knows anymore –
in a country occupied by
China, Japan, China.
Ask for fortune – you can buy
a paper one from the shops.
Edge round families picnicking
on mangoes and giant prawns.
Or praying. Then suddenly
the temple is roofless
hot evening flames your face.

Cross the width – wide
means important.
Wander walkways, punctuated
by Buddhas in wood cases carved
with dragons, birds, snakes.
Exit by the left door.
Leave behind your evil tigers.

In the Sarah P. Duke Gardens

No white candles open in spring
the old magnolia tree is dying.
Too many people have climbed it
torn its skin with triumphant feet;
its branches a stairwell in cool
green, a Jacob's ladder, tall
as Bath Abbey, levels signed
Kevin and Kimberley, Karen, Carl.
A large blue notice orders:
Do not climb. Do not carve.

Across the gardens, walkways
and mock orange lace new magnolia.
A man explains how he climbed
the magnolia with his two sons
each weekend visit.
Wisteria cloaks the gazebo.
In the pale linen evening sky
couples laze by the rose circle
two turtles mate on a stone by the lake
mosquitoes rise, and a boy climbs.

Headlines

In California the news is
Power Cuts Every Day.
There are too many air
conditioning and ice-making
machines. They de-regulated power –
my North Carolina friend laughs.
It didn't work. Contentedly
she sucks a fresh strawberry ice
clicks the automatic lock
of her long white Chevrolet.
But it's near crisis:
petrol will double in price.

Listening to God

at 105.7 FM. These twenty foot
letters gleam beside the Interstate.
It's just after *19 miles to Houston.*
On the other side, cars file homebound
for cold beer and dust-brown prairie.

Later, crackling across the dial
my fingers find the spot.
Hymn request hour is eight to ten.
'Our saviour is born'
'God is my rock', 'Alleluia'
pipes into cattle farms,
shanty-town shops,
and the Lone Star Brunch Bar
where Texans proudly read
how they are the fattest in the world.

It pipes here, into high rise rooms
competing against the all night
car-park elevator shafts,
and over the air-conditioning
and the Spanish speaking corridors
into the hospital, where Martin,
who has lost all understanding
of words and language,
hugs the family bible to his chest
and, somehow, is calmer.

Hurricane

It came on a chintzy day;
new walls painted,
pictures hung, wine cooled.
A carnival with friends
and presents and smiles
in shiny wrap to end
days of rented rooms,
cheapest margarine,
beans and acid fruit.

We didn't hear
the wind stir trees
misread gathered clouds,
our barometer long broken
radio off. Records blared
while the wind whipped
our straw bricks.

Landing was agony,
straining for air
under a crumpled
tissue of house;
uncovering
records scattered,
paintings shattered.
The sky arrogant blue.

Today, hot June ants crawl
over recently watered grass.
Their wings glint
like smudged glass.
This new house is fashioned
with mud and wood,
has a roof that rarely leaks.
But what is that rumble
in the distance?

Genoa Faces

for Massimo

1.
The first is you at the airport
face grey as linen.

I have not slept for three nights.

It looks like ten.

2.
My bag thuds into the car boot
and our talk turns to Primo Levi –
unable to return home after Auschwitz –
memories racking his skull
as he failed to cross the border.
Fumes rise on the autostrada.

They raided at 2 am.
The doors to the school
were locked.
For an hour, I heard their cries.
They would not let even
the doctors or lawyers in.

Not doctors or lawyers. Especially.
You remember the smell.

3.
My third is a two wheel rattling Vespa
a breeze that spears my jacket.

There were fifty in the schoolroom
Thirty are in hospital, broken arms,
legs, sleeping bags stuck
on bloodied skin.

We dodge mopeds and cars
between Christopher Columbus sea
and cinnamon mountains. I relish
the cascade of Bourgonvilia
recollect how the Genoese
were first to revolt against Hitler.
How are the nightmares
the voices weeping?

> *They came to our hospital –*
> *quickly, dress all the patients*
> *as doctors. Put on the soiled*
> *white coats.*

4.
The fourth is my mirror each morning.

> *Think. Who owns the TV*
> *the radio, the papers.*
> *You are surprised there is no news?*

I re-pot plants. New soil brings
variegated leaves, roots change.
I am moving to the sharp salty clay
of a cliff. It lacks nutrient, but survives
raw weather. Learning to grow on the edge
of a mountain where
purple thistles flourish.

5.
I hunt for broken windows
expected a city without water
riots, a burnt car on every corner.

> *They rose suddenly*
> *on the edge of the city –*
> *ten, or was it fifty, black dressed*
> *hoods, shirts, shoes? Marched four*
> *kilometers torching cars.*

The police watched.
We don't know who they were.
None of us wear black now.

After a week I found a broken window
recognised it from the Daily Mail
CNN, Corriere della Sera, each
photographed from a different angle.

Do you want to see the burnt car?

6.
The rest are rumours.

There was a place, out of the city
some were taken there.
After the crowd was stormed.

A German woman is missing.

We haven't been allowed there.

Someone saw her run over.

It happened just when the boy
was shot.

Are you sleeping yet?

No one can visit the one in hospital
who forfeited his spleen
half a lung.

Do you think you will be arrested?

I am going to recount this history
the disbelief of each face
as my story unfolded.

Those faces remembered are only
pale reflections of your face –
nights ransacked of sleep
the ruin of the city you love.

Replaying the Battle of Naseby

All night on my kitchen table
tiny roundhead generals
and cavaliers inspect their soldiers.
Foot soldiers were brown coated
torn trousered, couldn't afford
a uniform. Not like these

retrospective toys, 3 inch
high in red or blue or gold.
And pikes and muskets.
No dewy sweat
no wind stabs the sunken
backsides of weary horses.

All long day two lines
each razing each – sea and shore
horizon and sky, the scorched
end of a cannon. And for what?
All those dead and four hundred
years later to find

human shields, hostages, a bomb
wrecks the wrong country. Battle
is night raids from fifteen
thousand feet. Or refugees.
A custom of terror. Lying
is as easy as breathing

as we listen to our genes –
turn your hearing aid off, imagine
your eyelashes are glued shut
or admire the view elsewhere.
In the morning the kitchen table
grained with blood.

What the False Heart doth Know

Why have you taken to wearing silk
bold sequins of purple and gold?
Bangles scratch your starch arms
and when you lick your lips, your tongue
is sanded stone, sharp as dogfish.
Who dare not smile when you smile
not praise your high-backed chair
chink coins and compliments? Bacon
and oysters spice your breath. Growing
power. Seasons thinner by the hour.

Disturbing

I gaze out over this meadow's
salmon-coloured slender grasses.
Crickets hum, a reed warbler echoes.
Then a tooth-ache
in the lower jaw, an anxiety.
My lips recognise this dance.

Among mountains – slate sheer rocks
yellow plants burrowing
from blistered sun and jagged winds –
the memory recurs, sucking footsteps
a blister that rubs the swollen foot white
ankles weep, the tread learns to limp.

This many edged face
an argument both friend and enemy
a thief of pebbles in the green pond.
Even in brightest noon
a shadow pressing my shoulder
breathing loudly.

Legends and Dustbins

Open the window Marcus
let in the night breeze to quell
the fires of legends that flash
from your low voices. Apollo above
Cerberus below, the whole class of you
evening silhouettes at your oak table
in this oak panelled room. Port passes
to the left. From leather books
murmurs rise – Phaethon always the son
Hercules, Venus, Proserpina raped
the air heavy as Bacchus' wine.
Whatever folly you plot he will perform it.

Open the window Marcus
see those who scratch at hard earth
for fragments of history.
No soil to stick to the wrist as you dig.
No scheme of how it might have been
granite fort tops, mint grown
on the lower walls
tangerine cobbles that lead to a well.
No disappointment to spear your back
or to toss back to earth. Your family tree
hangs on the walls of this room.

Open the window Marcus
or have you learned ways to lock it closed?
At the corner of your meticulous garden
a woman searches dustbins
for scraps, she pulls at a newspaper
sucks dregs from a brandy bottle.

The grass sheds its colour
daffodils have turned their shoulders
distant thunder hums like gunfire
and the sky is hung with burnt out stars
fragments of methane and sulphur.
A barbarian breeze snakes over your arms.

Jackal at the Door

All night long there has been
a jackal at the door, watching for
my tread, howling, wolf constant,
its fur faking fox then pheasant,
crouched among autumn mulch.
Scent of dustbins.

                  I rise, look in the mirror.
Even the aspidistra is dying. Air
that no longer gives good blood
pumps in veins. Bone-hearted Gomorrah
weather. Streets complain of cancelled
busses, dangerous trains. Lights vanish
over the city. Then someone pours
petrol on the burning bush.

Waiting

The house is on fire, the books are on fire
my dreams are on fire. And I wake to
the constant image – a red passport,
bearing the photograph I took last week.
Authorised border papers.

As I dress, breakfast, walk –
rain slapping the hard asphalt
my mask like a black-jack player –
the left corner of my brain ticks,
packs my bags, selects the few special things

a perfume bottle, a white pebble,
an apple for the journey.
Guilty for those I leave
in the snarl of this country –
speech judged in the silence courts

appearance in the wage courts.
I fear the postman will steal my letters
listen for the whine of the gate
check the mail hourly. Dread
that the border will be sealed.

View from the Hill

for Franco

That was my street –
scent of bread baking
flour flaking from fingers
and outside showers on cobbles
pebble-dash houses
passages knitted in the dark
spaces between tenements.
And beyond, river –
coiling aloof from siesta walkers,
prams, fishermen knotted beside the bank –
heron, kingfisher, wren
calling all the colours of autumn.

I see it from this hill –
rediscover the small things
a look, a twisted smile, an innuendo.
Maybe it started then, maybe
it was always there –
invisible except in hindsight
a fault in the plates of earth
that one day shift, each
against each, leave us to
choose one side or the other
or fall between?

The inquisition was a shock.
Only after trials began
did I recognise indigo disappearances.
While new pirouettes of language
pumped over speakers
bewitching dogs, cats, tigers

to hound creatures at dusk
drag them to the town square.
All of us mesmerised
barking for retribution and blood
turning like a mongrel pack
between the murder of hyena or hare.

Then the blows arrived at my house.
We refugees carry so few possessions
over desert, hunger, thirst, pain –
and at the bottom of our bags
curled like a decayed bobbin –
guilt. Should I have stayed?
Others did, some became busy
fetching water, invented ways
to dissolve; some lived, died,
betrayed, swapped sides.

This is no movie of the Wild-West –
with dispositions all dagger,
all dove, all cloak, all book.
This is my street.
Rebuilt now
how will its history
be written –
veritas in dictis,
veritas in factis,
or veritas vitae?

War Museum on New Year's Day

He poses – shoulders
scraped back, five feet four –
beside the ten-meter 175-mm SFM 107 cannon.
She clicks the mini Canon camera shutter
thumb stiff from waiting.
Do not smile.

Across oceans my father
flicked the safety catch
of his battered gun,
aimed at rabbits for practice
and hunger.

Not this side   *but the other*
not my ancestor   *but his enemy*
not our dead   *but our killed.*

Her heels scuff marble floors
ache in Tokyo shoes
her pockets bulge with postcards
of fighter-bombers, submarine kamikazes
Samurai armour, the Divine Thunderbolt corps
in attack at Okinawa.

Not this attack   *another*
not their ancestor   *his enemy*
not their dead   *their killed.*

Out of the museum
the path threads past palmists,
noodle stalls, paper fortune sellers.
Ring the bell, wake the New Year god.

Beyond wide bronze gates
blacked-out mini-buses shout slogans
for lost lands.
A rabbit simmers on the stove.